KIDS LEARN TO

Crochet

07.
S.

KIDS LEARN TO

Crochet

Lucinda Guy & François Hall

Coats
Crafts UK

For all keen, new crocheters everywhere!

A Coats publication

This edition first published in 2008 by Coats Crafts UK
Lingfield House
Lingfield Point
McMullen Way
Darlington
Co. Durham DL1 1YJ

Technical consultant: Sally Harding

British Library Cataloguing in Publication Data
A catalogue record of this book is available from
the British Library

ISBN 978-1-906007-44-7

Reproduced and printed in Singapore

CONTENTS

WHAT IS CROCHET?

Crochet is a clever way of joining lots of **loops** of **yarn** together to make a piece of **fabric**. Crochet is made into all sorts of things that you can wear or use, like jumpers, blankets, bags and hats – or even posies of flowers!

Crocheting is very easy and anyone can do it. You just need to learn a few **basic stitches** and then **practise** them. It is as simple as that!

LET'S GET STARTED!

To start crocheting, all you need is some **yarn** and a **crochet hook**. Most yarns are made from wool or cotton and come in lots of different **colours** and textures, shapes and sizes.

There are also lots of **different sizes** of crochet hooks. The elephant is using a large, fat hook to crochet thick yarn with, and the bird is using a thin hook to crochet fine yarn with.

All the projects in this book are crocheted with a double-knitting yarn and a 4mm-sized hook.

THE SLIP KNOT

Choose some double-knitting yarn in a colour that you like – and let's get started on your very first piece of crochet!

The first thing you need to do is to attach the yarn to the crochet hook using a special knot, called a **slip knot**.

1

Start by making a **loop** in the yarn.

2 Take one end of the yarn and start to **pull** it through the loop that you have just made.

3 Now make a **another loop** that is big enough for the hook to **slide** right in.

4 Slide the hook through the loop that you have just made and pull the **short end** of the yarn tight. Next, pull the **ball end** of the yarn gently. Your **slip knot** is ready!

GET A GRIP!

Peg says:
Holding the yarn will feel strange to begin with but keep practising – your fingers will get used to it!

Before you can start crocheting you need to know how to **hold** your hook and yarn.

You use both hands to crochet. In this book we show the hook in the right hand and the yarn in the left hand. Don't worry if you are left handed – just switch left for right and right for left!

1 Hold the hook as shown using your thumb, forefinger (1) and middle finger (2).

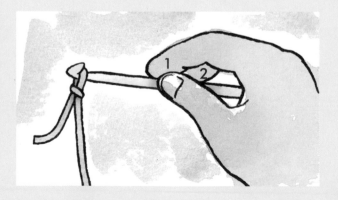

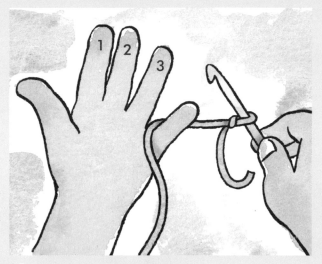

2 Now spread the fingers of your other hand, and catch the yarn with your little finger.

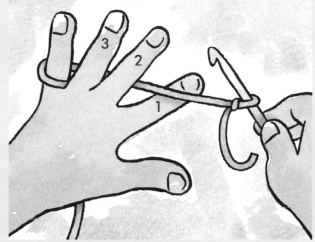

3 Turn your hand over, catching the yarn between fingers 1 and 2.

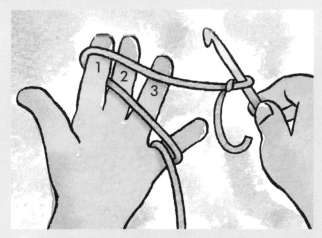

4 Turn your hand back. The yarn should now stretch from around your little finger, across fingers 3 and 2 and around the top of finger 1.

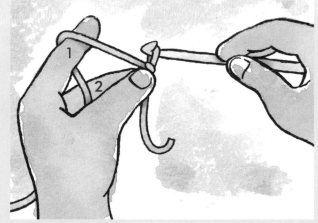

5 Keep finger 1 pointing up slightly, and use your thumb and finger 2 to hold onto the **slip knot**.

LET'S MAKE A CHAIN!

Now you are ready to learn how to use your crochet hook and yarn to make **lots of loops**, which are all joined together, one after the other to make a crochet chain. These loops are called **chain stitches**.

The longer your starting chain, the wider your crochet will be.

Peg says:

Practise making lots of chain stitches and see how long you can make your chain. You can use your chain to tie up presents, put in your hair or stitch to your crochet as decoration.

The **front** of your chain looks like this – each chain stitch looks like a 'V'. You can count the number of stitches you have made by counting the 'V's.

1
2
3
4
5
6
7
8
9
10
11

The **back** of your chain looks like this – it's bumpy and you can't see any 'V's.

15

1

With your hook and yarn in position, push the hook underneath and around the yarn following the arrow.

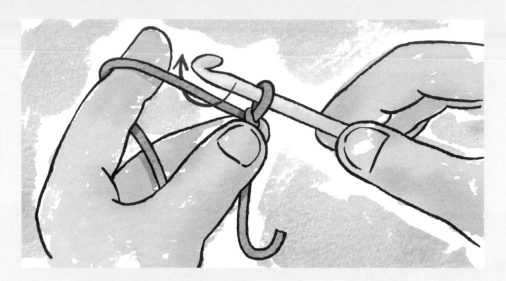

2

Catch the yarn with the tip of the hook.

Pip says:

Count the stitches as you make your chain, and write down the number so you don't forget.

Check how you are holding the yarn – make sure your chain stitches are not too loose or too tight.

3

Carefully pull the **hook and yarn** back through the slip knot on the hook.

Try to keep the hook facing downwards so the yarn does not slip off the hook.

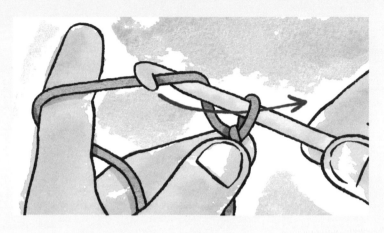

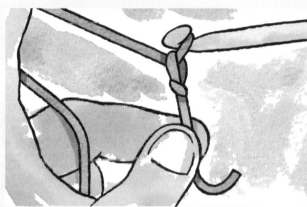

4

Well done, you have just made your first **chain stitch!**

5

Repeat steps 1–3 to make more chain stitches.

Move your thumb and middle finger up the chain **closer** to the hook as you make more stitches.

DOUBLE CROCHET

Once you have practised making a crochet chain, and can create a chain with nice even stitches, you are ready to learn your first crochet stitch – the **double crochet stitch**.

Let's get crocheting!

Peg says:

Take your time and make sure you are holding your hook and yarn right – if you are holding the yarn too tightly, your stitches will be too tight as well, and difficult to crochet into. Just keep practising!

The front and back look just the same!

19

Your first row

Make a slip knot, and slip it onto your hook. Get your hook and yarn in position and make a chain of **11 chain stitches**. Then pick up your chain and hold it on its side so that it looks like this.

The yarn tail is now at the left end of the chain and the yarn from your ball of yarn, which you will crochet with, is now on the right.

1

Skipping over the first chain stitch next to the hook, push the hook through the centre of the **second chain stitch** from the hook.

Pip says:
Make sure you have the front of the chain facing you so you can see each stitch like a 'V' – not the back, which looks all bumpy.

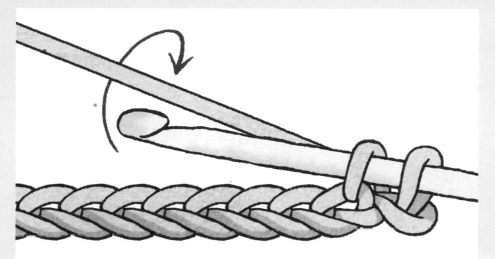

2
Push the hook underneath and around the yarn.

3
Catch the yarn with the tip of the hook, and pull the hook and yarn through the chain stitch nearest the tip of the hook.

4
You now have **two loops** on your hook – the loop you have just made and the last stitch of your long chain.

5
Catch the yarn in the tip of the hook again, and carefully pull it through **both loops** on your hook.

6
Well done, you have just made your first **double crochet stitch!**

7
Now finish your row by making a double crochet stitch into the next and all the other chain stitches. To do this, repeat steps 1–5 into each of your chain stitches.

When you have finished your **first row** of double crochet, take a good look at the stitches that you have just made. You can see that the top of each double crochet stitch is shaped like a 'V'.

Count each 'V' to make sure you have the right number of stitches.

If you started with a chain of **11 chain stitches**, you should now have **10 double crochet stitches** – this is because you skipped over the first chain stitch when you started your row.

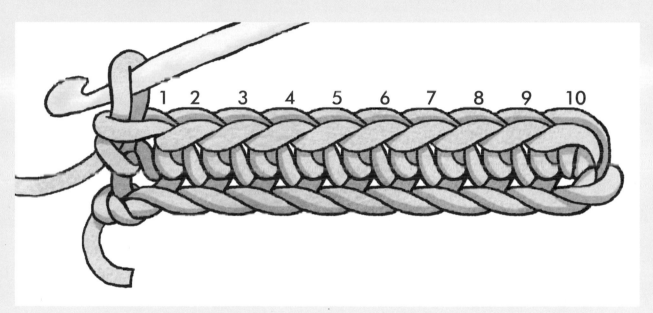

Peg says:

If you make 21 chain stitches, you will have 20 double crochet stitches in your first row.

How many double crochet stitches will you have in your first row if you made 101 chain stitches? (100!)

Turning your crochet

You have finished your first row of double crochet, and you are now ready to start your **second row**.

But first, **turn** your piece of crochet around.

The yarn tail will now be at the bottom right corner of your crochet and the yarn attached to the ball of yarn will be at the top, on the right.

Before you turn your crochet...

Pip says:

At the beginning of all odd rows (rows 1, 3, 5, 7 and 9)
the yarn and the yarn tail will be on the left!

At the beginning of all even rows (rows 2, 4, 6, 8 and 10)
the yarn and the yarn tail will be on the right!

... and after you turn your crochet.

Your second row

1

Have your hook, yarn and crochet in position and make **one chain stitch**.

2

Make a double crochet stitch into the **top** of the first stitch in the row below, making sure that you push the hook right under the 'V' of the stitch.

Peg says:
Each time you start a double crochet stitch, make sure you push your hook right under the 'V' of the top of the stitch in the row below.

3

Make a double crochet stitch into the next and every stitch all the way along your piece of crochet, right back to the very first double crochet stitch that you made.

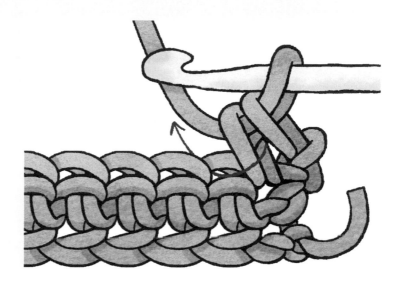

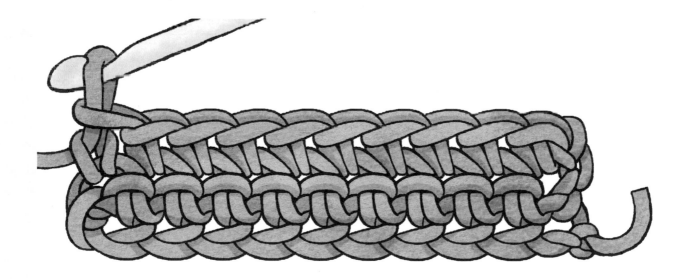

4

You have now finished your **second row**!

Keep making rows of crochet in exactly the same way, and remember to **turn** your crochet and make **one chain** each time you start a new row!

HOW TO **STOP** CROCHETING

Fastening off stops your crochet from coming undone!

When you have made as many rows of crochet as you want, you need to know how to stop crocheting.

This is called **fastening off**.

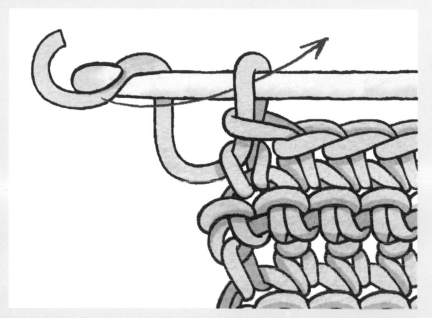

1

Once you have finished the last stitch on your last row, cut the yarn leaving a long tail. Then use the crochet hook to pull the yarn tail right **through the loop**.

2

With your fingers, pull the yarn tail **tight** to close the loop.

You have finished **fastening off**!

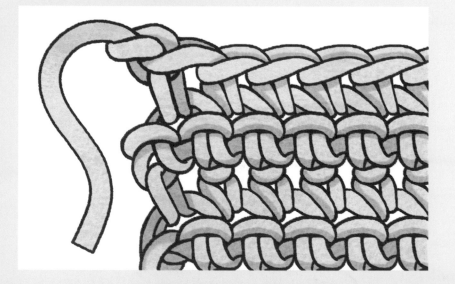

GET THE
SIZE RIGHT

You know that starting with lots of chain stitches makes a **wide piece** of crochet, and starting with just a few chain stitches makes a **narrow piece** of crochet.

To make your crochet just the **right size**, you will need to follow a **crochet pattern** that tells you exactly how many chain stitches you need to make and how many rows you need to crochet. The easiest kind of pattern to follow is a **chart**.

Once you know how to follow a chart you can crochet all the great projects in this book.

Each coloured **square** on this chart equals one double crochet stitch.

If a chart is 12 squares wide, like the one here, you need to make a chain of 13 stitches, so that you will have 12 stitches at the end of the first row. If it is 12 squares high, you need to crochet 12 rows.

The squares are very small – so if you find it hard to read your chart, ask someone to photocopy it and make it bigger.

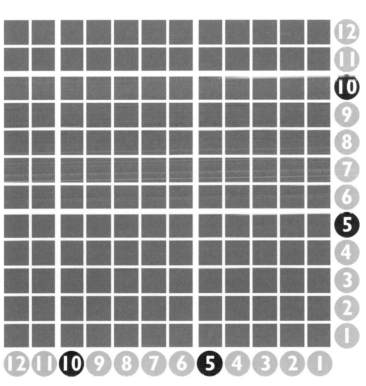

Peg says:
The squares up the side of the chart show how many rows you need to crochet.

Pip says:
The squares across the bottom of the chart show how many stitches you will have after your first row of crochet.

To help you keep track of how many rows you have crocheted, photocopy your chart and draw a pencil line across it each time you finish a row.

Before you start crocheting, make sure you have made the right number of chain stitches. Then count your stitches after every few rows to make sure you have the right number.

33

Beaky George is quick and fun to make using the **double crochet stitch.** George likes to sit on top of your pen or pencil, or on your finger. Why not make **lots of friends** for Beaky George – one for each finger and thumb?

Making George

George is made from just one piece of crochet. His head feathers are made from yellow felt, and his beak from blue felt. His eye is a button stitched onto orange felt.

To crochet George

Follow the chart to crochet George to the right size. There are 10 squares across the bottom of the chart – so using blue yarn, make a chain of 11 stitches so that you will have 10 double crochet stitches in your first row. The chart is 10 squares high – so you will need to crochet 10 rows using the double crochet stitch.

When you have finished crocheting, fasten off (see page 29).

Sew in any yarn ends (see page 91).

Chart

You will need

- One ball of double-knitting yarn in blue
- 4mm crochet hook
- Yellow, blue and orange felt
- One button for George's eye

Putting George together

Fold your piece of crochet in half and stitch it together along the two side edges to make a tube (see page 89).

Sew in any yarn ends (see page 91).

Felt shapes for George

Use the templates on page 93 to cut out George's beak, eye and head feathers. You need to cut down the lines of the head feathers. Ask someone to help you cut out the pieces and stitch them to George. You will also need one button for George's eye.

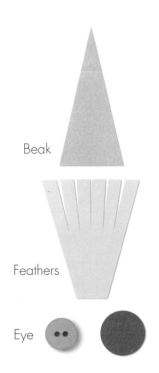

Beak

Feathers

Eye

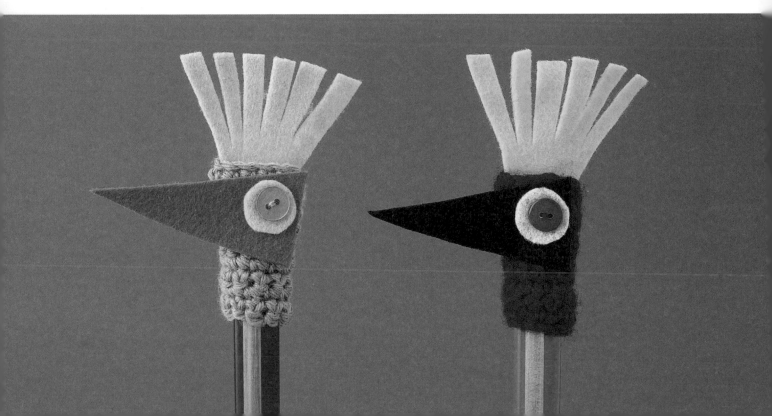

FEATHERY FRANK

EARLY BIRD ERIC

Sew on the felt shapes and the button (see page 92). Put the bottom edge of the head feathers **down inside** the crochet tube. Then put the beak, orange felt and button eye in position. Stitch the felt circle and button onto George's beak, making sure the stitches go through both sides of the crochet and the head feathers inside, as well as the beak.

Make George some friends

You can make Beaky George some friends by using different coloured yarns and felt.

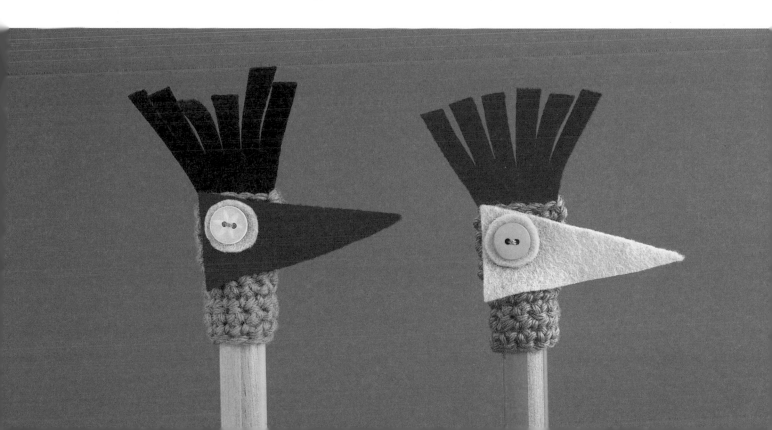

CROCHETING WITH STRIPES

Crocheting with lots of **different colours** of yarn can be really fun. The more colours you use, the more exciting your crochet will look!

You can have **wide stripes** or **narrow stripes** – or even a mix of wide and narrow stripes in the same piece of crochet.

Pip says:
When you make stripes of colour, you have to join in each new colour of yarn carefully. It is easier to start a new colour at the end of a row than in the middle or at the beginning.

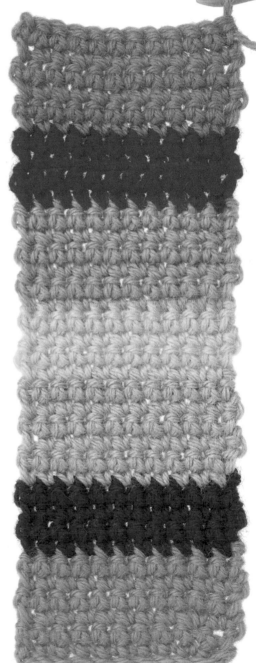

...and big wide ones!

Lots of small narrow stripes...

1 To join in a **new colour** of yarn, cut the yarn you have been crocheting with – about 10cm from your last stitch.

2 Take the new colour and wrap it around the hook, leaving a tail about 10cm long.

3 Pull the new yarn colour through the loop on the hook.

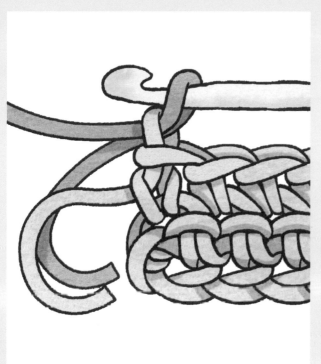

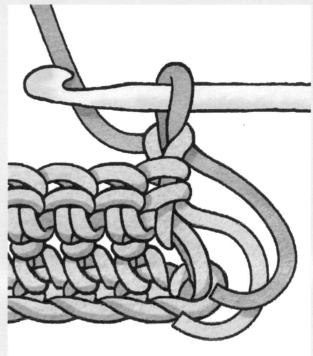

4

Give the old yarn colour a **tug** – this will tighten the stitch and help keep the new yarn colour in place.

5

Turn your crochet. You are now ready to start crocheting with your new yarn colour!

Peg says:

If you want to make lots of different coloured stripes of crochet, you will get lots of yarn ends dangling from your crochet. Don't worry about these as you can hide them later by sewing them into the wrong side (see page 91).

2

Gorgeous Stripy Stu is easy to make in **double crochet** with simple red stripes. You can also make **lots of friends** for him.

Get crocheting!

Making Stripy Stu

Stripy Stu's body is made from just two pieces of crochet. His ears, tail, feet and whiskers are made from yellow felt and his tongue from red felt. He has a big button for his nose and two small buttons stitched onto blue felt for his eyes.

To crochet Stripy Stu's body

Stu's body is made in two pieces of double crochet, both the same size.

Using red yarn, make a chain of 15 stitches so that you will have 14 double crochet stitches in your first row.

Follow the chart carefully, changing the yarn colour from red to beige as shown on the chart.

When you have finished crocheting all 26 rows, fasten off (see page 29).

Sew in any yarn ends (see page 91).

Make another piece of crochet just the same for the other side of Stu's body.

Chart

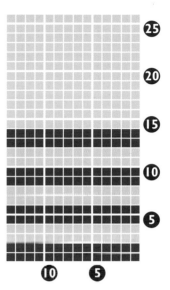

You will need

- Two balls of double-knitting yarn – one red and one beige
- 4mm crochet hook
- Yellow, red and blue felt
- One big button for Stu's nose
- Two small buttons for Stu's eyes
- Toy filling

WHISKERY WALTER
14 stitches and 26 rows

FURRY FRED
12 stitches and 30 rows

BIG BERT
16 stitches and 20 rows

PURRING PETE
12 stitches and 34 rows

Putting Stripy Stu together

Put the two pieces of crochet together and stitch them along three sides (see page 89).

Put in the toy filling, then sew the opening closed (see page 90).

Sew in any yarn ends (see page 91).

Felt shapes for Stripy Stu

Use the templates on page 94 to make Stu's ears, tail, feet, whiskers, tongue and eyes. Ask someone to help you cut them out and stitch them to Stu's body (see page 92). You will also need three buttons for Stu's nose and eyes.

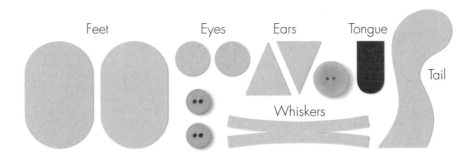

Feet   Eyes   Ears   Tongue   Tail   Whiskers

Make Stripy Stu some friends!

You can make Stu some friends in different sizes, stripes and colours. Just work each of the two pieces of crochet in the number of stitches and rows given on the left.

CROCHETING SHAPES

You can make your crochet **narrower** by decreasing (taking stitches away) or **wider** by increasing (adding stitches).

Until now, you have only made things with straight sides. When you have learned how to decrease and increase, you will be able to crochet **different shapes**.

Peg says:
If you decrease or increase stitches at the beginning and at the end of every row, or every other row, you can make a triangle.

Decreasing (making your crochet narrower)

Make a slip knot and slip it onto your hook. Get your hook and yarn in position and make a chain of 11 stitches. Then crochet two rows of double crochet. The easiest way to decrease is to crochet together the first two stitches at the beginning and end of the row.

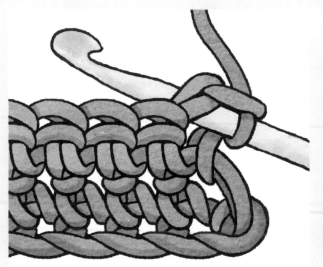

1

Make one chain stitch at the beginning of your decrease row.

Then push the hook through the top of the first stitch in the row below.

2

Push the hook underneath and around the yarn, catching the yarn in the tip of the hook.

Then pull the hook and yarn through the stitch in the row below.

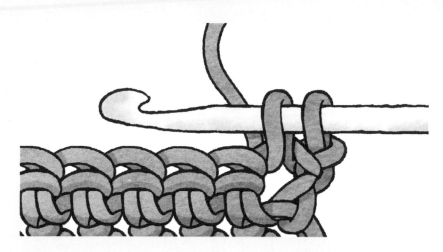

3

You now have **two loops** on your hook.

4

Push the hook through the top of the next stitch in the row below.

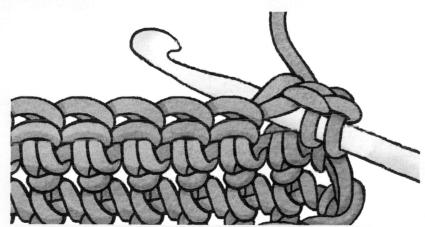

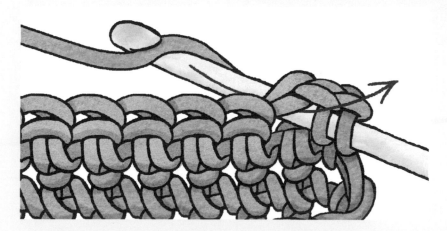

5

Catch the yarn with the tip of the hook, and pull the hook and yarn through the second stitch in the row below.

6

You now have **three loops** on your hook.

7

Catch the yarn with the tip of the hook again, and pull the hook and yarn through **all three loops** on your hook.

8

You have just made **one decrease**!

Crochet six double crochet stitches, then make **one more decrease** at the end of the row by crocheting the last two stitches together.

Count your stitches. You should now have **eight stitches** – two less than you started with!

Increasing (making your crochet wider)

Make a slip knot and slip it onto your hook. Get your hook and yarn in position and make a chain of 11 stitches. Then crochet two rows of double crochet. The easiest way to increase is to crochet into the same stitch twice at the beginning and end of the row.

1　Make one chain at the start of the increase row. Then make one double crochet stitch into the first stitch in the row below.

2　Make one more double crochet stitch in exactly the same stitch in the row below.

3　You have just made **one increase**!

Crochet eight double crochet stitches, then make **one more increase** at the end of the row by crocheting two stitches into the last stitch.

Count your stitches. You should now have **twelve stitches** – two more than you started with!

Practise your **decreasing** and **increasing** skills by crocheting Sweet Mousie and all her little friends.

Making Sweet Mousie

Sweet Mousie's body is made with one piece of crochet. Her nose, whiskers, arms, feet and outer ears are made from blue felt, and her inner ears and eyes are made from pink felt. She has one small button stitched onto the end of her nose and two small buttons stitched onto pink felt for her eyes. Her tail is made from a crochet chain.

To crochet Mousie's body

To make Mousie, you will first need to decrease stitches and then increase stitches (see pages 48–51).

Follow the chart carefully. Remember to change your yarn colour on row 11 as shown on the chart.

Using navy yarn, make a chain of 21 stitches so that you will have 20 double crochet stitches in your first row. Crochet 2 rows of double crochet. On the next row (**row 3**), decrease one stitch at each end of the row as shown on the chart.

Chart

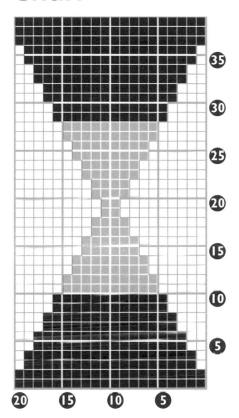

You will need

- Two balls of double-knitting yarn – one navy and one green
- 4mm crochet hook
- Blue and pink felt
- Two buttons for Mousie's eyes
- One button for Mousie's nose
- Toy filling

Crochet the next row without decreasing any stitches. Follow the chart, decreasing one stitch at each end of every other row until you have 2 crochet stitches. Crochet one more row (**row 20**).

WEE MYRTLE

On the next row (**row 21**), increase one stitch at each end of the row. Crochet the next row without increasing any stitches. Follow the chart, increasing one stitch at each end of every other row, until you have 20 stitches and have finished row 39. Remember to change your yarn colour on row 29 as shown on the chart.

Fasten off (see page 29).

Sew in any yarn ends (see page 91).

Making Mousie's tail

Using navy yarn, make a chain of 30 stitches and fasten off.

LITTLE LOTTIE

Putting Mousie together

Fold your crochet in half and stitch the two sides together (see page 89). Put in the toy filling, then sew the opening closed (see page 90).

Sew one end of Mousie's tail onto her back, in the middle on the lower edge.

Make a knot with the yarn tail on the end of Mousie's tail and trim.

Sew in any yarn ends (see page 91).

Felt shapes for Mousie

Use the templates on page 94 to make Mousie's nose, whiskers, inner and outer ears, arms, feet and eyes. Ask someone to help you cut them out and stitch them to Mousie's body (see page 92).

You will also need one button for Mousie's nose and two for her eyes.

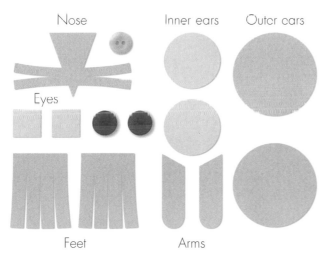

Nose   Inner ears   Outer ears

Eyes

Feet   Arms

Make Mousie some friends!

You can make Mousie some friends by using different colours of yarn and felt.

TREBLE
CROCHET

Now it's time to learn another stitch! This one is called the **treble crochet stitch.** It's very like the double crochet stitch, so you will find it easy to learn. It makes a nice **open fabric** that grows quickly.

Get practising and you will be making treble crochet stitches in no time!

The front and back look just the same!

Make a slip knot and slip it onto your hook. Get your hook and yarn in position and make a chain of 12 stitches. Then pick the chain up and hold it so that it is on its side ready to start the first row.

When making your first treble crochet, you skip over the last three chain stitches that you made and make your first stitch into the fourth chain stitch from the hook.

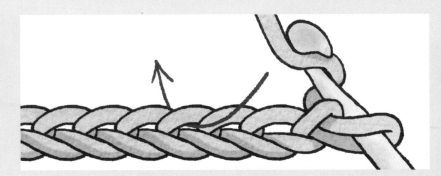

1 Wrap the yarn around your hook. (The arrow shows where you are going to put your hook for your first stitch.)

2 Skipping over the first three chain stitches, push the hook through the centre of the **fourth chain stitch** from the hook.

3 Push the hook underneath and around the yarn, and pull the hook and yarn through the chain stitch.

4

You now have **three loops** on your hook – the two loops you have just made and the last stitch of the long chain.

5

Push the hook underneath and around the yarn again, and pull the hook and yarn through the **first two loops** on your hook.

6

You now have **two loops** on your hook.

7

Push the hook underneath and around the yarn again, and pull the hook and yarn through **both the loops** on your hook.

8

You have just made your first **treble crochet stitch!**

It's a very tall stitch, isn't it!

9

Repeat steps 1–7 into the next and all the other chain stitches to finish your **first row**.

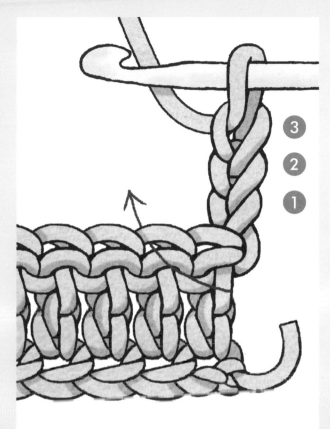

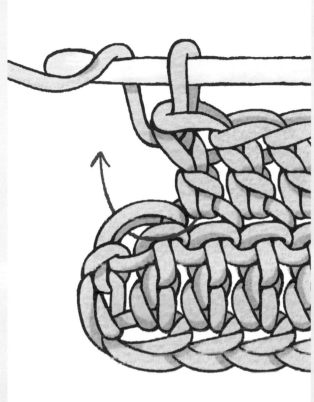

10

Turn your crochet ready to start your **second row**.

Make three chain stitches – these count as your first treble crochet stitch in the row. Then skip the first stitch in the row below and make your first **real** treble crochet in the next stitch, inserting the hook under the 'V' (see page 26).

11

Crochet seven more treble crochet stitches.

Then make the last treble crochet stitch into the third of the three chain stitches in the row below.

Repeat steps 10–11 for all the following rows. You now have ten treble crochet stitches in your row.

4

This lovely little Best Bag is made using the **treble crochet stitch**. It is very easy to make and **very useful** to have. Get crocheting and you will be using it in no time!

Making the Best Bag

The bag is crocheted in one piece of treble crochet, with two narrow turquoise stripes and one wide blue stripe.

The handle is made with just one row of treble crochet and two buttons for decoration. The flower is made with red felt, decorated with a circle of blue felt and a button.

To crochet the Best Bag

Using turquoise yarn, make a chain of 20 stitches so that you will have 18 stitches in your first row. (Remember, the first 3 chain stitches of every row count as the first treble crochet stitch of the row.)

Crochet 3 rows of treble crochet as shown on the chart.

Change to blue yarn and crochet 12 rows of treble crochet as shown on the chart.

Change to turquoise yarn and crochet 3 rows of treble crochet as shown on the chart.

Fasten off (see page 28).

Sew in any yarn ends (see page 91).

Chart

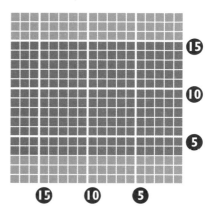

You will need

- Two balls of double-knitting yarn – one blue and one turquoise
- 4mm crochet hook
- Red and blue felt
- Three buttons for decoration

To crochet the bag handle

Make a chain of 40 stitches and crochet one row of treble crochet. Fasten off (see page 29).

Sew in any yarn ends (see page 91).

Putting the bag together

Fold your piece of crochet in half and stitch it together along both sides (see page 89). Stitch the handle to the sides of the bag. Sew on the two buttons (see page 92).

Felt shapes for the bag

Use the templates on page 93 to make the felt flower. Ask someone to help you cut out the pieces and stitch them to your bag (see page 92). You will need a button to decorate the flower.

Petal

Flower centre

Buttons for decoration

Make lots of bags for your friends!

You can make lots of bags – just change the colour of the yarn and felt to make them look different.

CROCHETING IN CIRCLES

So far you have learnt how to crochet in **rows**, where you turn the crochet every time you finish a row to start a new one. When you crochet in **circles**, you crochet **round and round** without turning.

You can also use lots of different coloured yarns and make **stripy circles**.

Let's get started!

Make a slip knot and slip it onto your hook.
Then get your hook and yarn in position.

1

Make two chain stitches.

2

Skip over the first chain stitch and make
one double crochet stitch into the
second chain stitch from the hook.

3

Make five more double
crochet stitches into
the centre of the same
chain stitch.

Try to keep the yarn tail out
of the way at the back of
your crochet – you don't
want to it to get caught up
in your stitches!

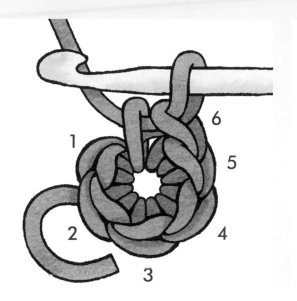

4

You have now made six double crochet stitches.

You have finished **round 1**!

5

To help keep track of your rounds, you need to use a **stitch marker**.

Every time you finish a round, move the stitch marker onto the last stitch you made to mark the end of that round.

To help you understand how crochet rounds are made, look at the chart on the right.

The stitches for **round 1** are shown as six blue dots – each dot equals one stitch.

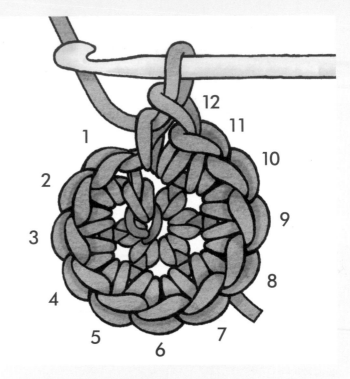

6   In **round 2**, you will need to increase the number of your stitches to make your circle bigger.

Make two double crochet stitches into the next stitch – this makes **one increased stitch**.

7   Make one increase into **every stitch** all the way around your circle, back to the last stitch with the marker on it.

You have just made 12 stitches. 6 stitches + 6 increases = 12 stitches.

This chart shows you where the increases are made. The stitches in **round 2** are shown as 12 green dots – each dot equals one stitch.

You can see that you increase the number of your stitches by making two stitches into each one of the six stitches of the first round.

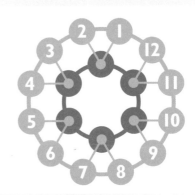

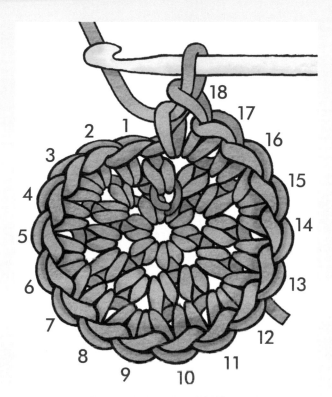

Before you start **round 3**, move the stitch marker onto the last stitch you made.

In this round you only make one increase into **every other stitch**. To do this, make one double crochet stitch into the first stitch, then make one increase – two double crochets – into the next stitch. Keep doing this all the way around, back to the marker.

You should now have 18 stitches. 12 stitches + 6 increases = 18

This chart shows you where the increases are made in **round 3**.

The stitches in round 3 are shown as 18 red dots.

You can see that you increase the number of your stitches by making two stitches into every other one of the 12 green stitches of round 2.

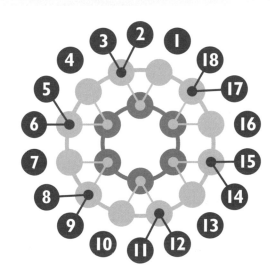

Fastening off

When your circle is big enough and you have made your last stitch on your last round, you need to **fasten off**.

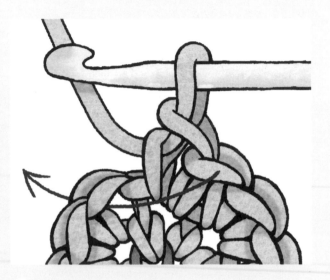

1

Make one double crochet stitch into the next stitch.

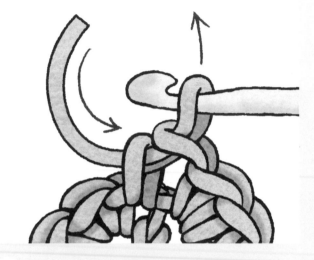

2

Cut the yarn, leaving a **long tail**, and use the hook to pull the yarn tail right through the loop on the hook.

3

With your fingers, pull the yarn tail **tight** to close the last loop.

Your circle is fastened off and **safe** from coming undone!

Making bigger circles

If you want to make your crochet circle bigger, you just need to keep making rounds of double crochet, increasing stitches on every round.

For every new round that you crochet, you will need to add one to the number of stitches you make before making an increase.

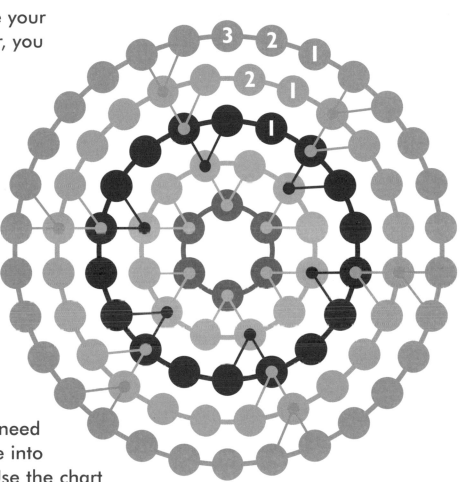

So, if you make a **fourth round**, you need to make an increase into every **third** stitch. Use the chart and follow the pink dots to help you keep count of your increases and stitches.

If you make a **fifth round**, you need to make an increase into every **fourth** stitch – follow the light blue dots to help you keep count of your increases and stitches.

See how many rounds you can crochet!

Making a stripy circle

You can have lots of fun using different colours and crocheting stripy circles. You can use a different colour for each round!

1

Make two rounds of double crochet, following steps 1–7 on pages 68–70.

When you are making the last double crochet stitch in your second round, **stop** halfway through the stitch – when you still have two loops on your hook.

Cut the old yarn, leaving a long tail at the back of your circle, and wrap your new yarn around the hook.

Peg says:

If you use a different colour for each round, it makes it easier to count your stitches and increases, and keep track of where you are!

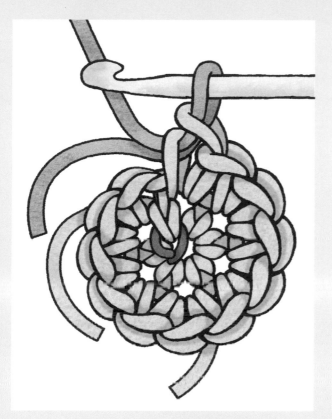

2

Then pull the new yarn through the two loops on your hook, leaving a long tail.

You have just finished your last double crochet stitch using your new colour!

Give the yarn ends a gentle **tug** to tighten the stitch.

3

Crochet **round 3** by following step 8 on page 71.

You have crocheted one round in your new colour!

When you have finished making your stripy circle, fasten off (see page 72).

These Fabulous Flowers are fun and quick to make in just a few simple, stripy rounds of **double crochet**. They will look lovely as a brooch or as decoration for a **present**. Get crocheting and see how many you can make!

Making the flower

The flower is crocheted in one piece, using double crochet. The petals of the flower are made in blue and red felt. You will need one button for the centre.

To crochet the flower

Using pink yarn, make a chain of 2 stitches.

Make 6 double crochet stitches into the second chain stitch from the hook.

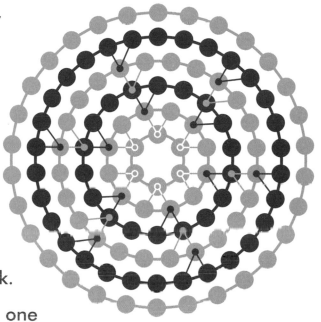

Following the chart carefully, crochet one more round, increasing one into every stitch as the chart shows. You should now have **12 stitches** on your circle.

Change to red yarn and crochet one more round, increasing one into every other stitch as the chart shows. You should now have **18 stitches**.

Change to pink yarn and crochet one more round, increasing one into every 3rd stitch as the chart shows. You should now have **24 stitches** on your circle.

You will need

- Two balls of double-knitting yarn – one pink and one red
- 4mm crochet hook
- Blue and red felt
- One button for flower centre

Change to red yarn and crochet one more round, increasing one into every 4th stitch as the chart shows. You should now have **30 stitches** on your circle.

Change to pink yarn and crochet one more round without any increasing as the chart shows.

Fasten off (see page 72).

Sew in any ends (see page 91).

Felt shapes for the flower

Use the templates on page 93 to make two petals. Ask someone to help you cut them out and stitch them to your crocheted flower. You will also need a button for the centre.

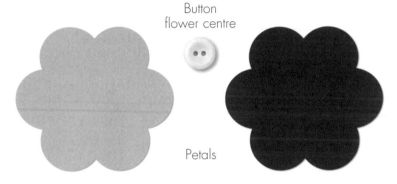

Button flower centre

Petals

Putting the flower together

Lay the blue felt petal on top of the red felt petal and then put the crochet circle on top of the felt. Stitch the button in place (see page 92). Make sure you stitch through the crochet, the blue felt and the red felt!

Make lots of Fabulous Flowers

Make lots of Fabulous Flowers by using different coloured yarn and felt.

Make handsome All-Together Albert and give yourself a chance to **practise everything** you have learnt so far – **all together** in one project!

Making Albert

Chart 1

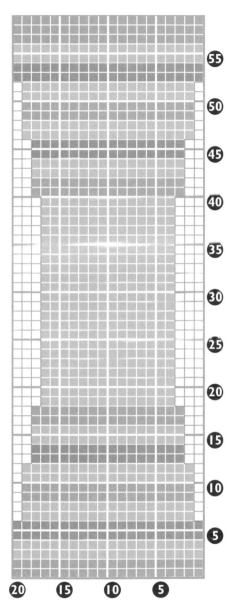

Albert's body is made in one piece using double crochet. His ears are circles made using the double crochet stitch, and his scarf is made in one piece using treble crochet. His nose is made from blue felt, and his arms and feet are made from orange felt. He has a button stitched onto blue felt for each eye.

To crochet Albert's body

To make Albert, you will need to first decrease stitches and then increase stitches (see pages 48–51), making stripes at the same time (see pages 40–41).

Follow Chart 2 carefully for Albert's body.

You will need

- Three balls of double-knitting yarn – one green, one turquoise and one beige
- 4mm crochet hook
- Blue and orange felt
- Two buttons for Albert's eyes
- Toy filling

Chart 2

Using green yarn, make a chain of 21 stitches so that you will have 20 stitches in your first row. Crochet 2 rows of double crochet. On the next row (row 3), change to beige yarn and crochet 2 rows. Change to turquoise yarn and crochet 2 rows as the chart shows.

On the next row (row 7), change to beige yarn and decrease one stitch at each end of the row. Crochet the next row without decreasing. Following the chart carefully for the colours, decrease on every 6th row until row 19.

Crochet up to row 40 to make Albert's upper body and head.

On the next row (**row 41**), change to green yarn and increase one stitch at each end of the row. Crochet the next row without increasing any stitches.

Following the chart carefully for the colours, increase one stitch at each end of every 6th row until you have 20 stitches again and have finished row 59.

Fasten off (see page 29).

Sew in any yarn ends (see page 91).

Making Albert's ears

Using turquoise yarn, make a chain of 2 stitches.

Make 6 double crochet stitches into the second chain stitch from the hook.

Following Chart 1 carefully (see page 81), crochet one more round, increasing one into every stitch as the chart shows. You should now have **12 stitches**.

Fasten off (see page 72).

Making Albert's scarf

Using turquoise yarn, make a chain of 60 stitches and crochet one row of treble crochet. Fasten off (see page 29).

Putting Albert together

Fold your piece of crochet in half and stitch the two sides together (see page 89). Put in the toy filling, then sew the opening closed (see page 90). Sew on Albert's ears as shown in the photo.

Sew in any yarn ends (see page 91).

Wrap Albert's scarf around his neck.

Felt shapes for Albert.

Use the templates on page 94 to make Albert's nose, eyes, arms and feet. Ask someone to help you cut them out and stitch them to Albert's body (see page 92). You will also need two buttons for Albert's eyes.

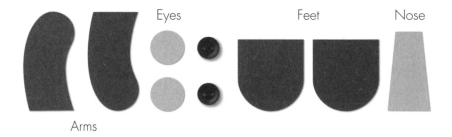

Eyes   Feet   Nose

Arms

Make Albert some friends

You can make Albert some friends by using different colours of yarn and felt.

WHEN THINGS GO WRONG

You have been learning lots of new things about **crochet** and **practising** hard – but what can you do if your crochet doesn't look right?

No problem! There are things that can go wrong, but they are **easy to fix**.

Too tight?

If your crochet looks too small and tight, you may be crocheting too tightly. Make sure you are holding your hook and yarn right and relax! You could try using a slightly bigger hook. Go slowly and try to make each stitch carefully!

Too loose?

If your crochet looks too big and loose, you may be crocheting too loosely. Make sure you are holding your hook and yarn right and that the yarn is running through your fingers as you have learnt. Make each stitch carefully. You could also try using a slightly smaller crochet hook. Just keep practising and you will get it right!

You have used all your yarn

If you have been busily crocheting and all your yarn is gone, you will need to start a new ball and join it to your crochet. You can do this just as you did when you joined in a different colour of yarn for stripy crochet on pages 40 and 41.

Always try and remember to join in the new yarn at the end of the row, as it is easier to do it there.

Missed stitches

You can tell if you have missed a stitch by counting them – if you were crocheting with 20 stitches and you crochet a row and find that you can only count 19, you have missed a stitch. This is quite easy to do when you are learning how to crochet as it can be difficult sometimes to see where to put your hook to make a new stitch.

Sometimes you can miss more than one stitch. You may notice that your crochet is becoming a funny shape and sloping in at the sides.

Too many stitches

You may notice that you have got more stitches at the end of the row then you should have. It can be difficult sometimes to see where to put your hook to make a new stitch and you end up making more stitches in the wrong place.

If you have the wrong number of stitches, you will need to unravel the row of crochet you have just made and start from the beginning again!

HOW TO...

Stitch seams

Things that are made in two pieces, or folded in half, need to be stitched together at the edges. This is called a seam. You will need some pins, a large sewing needle threaded with yarn and a pair of scissors. Always get someone to help with your sewing or let them do it for you.

1. Pin together the pieces of crochet. Make sure that the sides you want for the right sides are facing each other and the wrong sides are facing outwards. If you are sewing together striped pieces, make sure you are using matching sides for the right side of the crochet!

2. Push the needle and yarn through both layers close to the edge, leaving a long yarn tail. Make one stitch and push the needle back through the crochet. Continue until you have sewn all the seams you need to. Remove the pins and sew in any yarn ends (see page 91).

Fill toys

Soft toys like Stripy Stu (page 42) and Sweet Mousie (page 52) need to be stuffed with toy filling to make them cuddly. You will need some pins, a large sewing needle threaded with yarn, some toy filling and a pair of scissors.

1 Stitch the pieces of crochet together along the sides, leaving one side open (see page 89). Then turn the knitting right side out.

2 Take a handful of toy filling and fill the crocheted shape. Use just enough filling to make the toy look plump but not fat.

3 Stitch together the open side to close it, as shown in the photo, and sew in any yarn ends (see page 91).

Peg says:
To sew on buttons and felt shapes, you will need some fine yarn. Cut a length of double-knitting yarn and untwist it to make two lengths. Then use one length as your sewing thread.

Sew in yarn ends

To make your crochet look nice and neat, you need to tidy up any loose yarn ends. If you have been making lots of stripes, you will have lots of yarn ends. Sew in all the ends in the same way.

1 Thread the yarn end onto a large sewing needle and pass the needle under and over several of the nearest stitches on the back of the crochet, along the edge (or down the stripe).

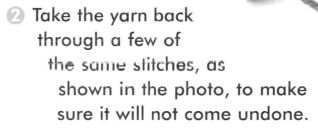

2 Take the yarn back through a few of the same stitches, as shown in the photo, to make sure it will not come undone.

91

Stitch felt shapes to crochet

You will need a large sewing needle threaded with fine yarn and a pair of scissors.

1 Place the felt shape on your crochet and push the needle and yarn through both the crochet and the felt from the back, leaving a long tail of yarn.

2 Push the needle back through the felt and the crochet, as shown in the photo. You may need to do this several times.

Knot the yarn ends at the back and trim them.

Sew on buttons

You can do this with just one stitch. You will need a large sewing needle threaded with fine yarn and a pair of scissors.

1 Place the felt on the crochet, with the button on top. Push the needle and yarn through from the back so that they go right through the crochet, the felt and the button, leaving a long tail of yarn.

2 Push the needle back through the button, felt and crochet. Knot the yarn ends at the back and trim them.

TEMPLATES

Beaky George
(page 34)

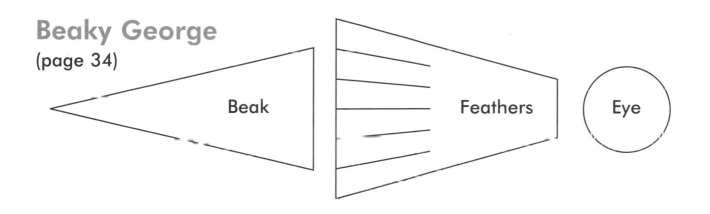

Beak

Feathers

Eye

Best Bag (page 62)

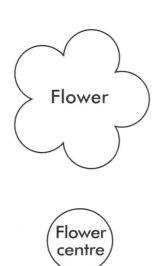

Flower

Flower centre

Fabulous Flowers (page 76)

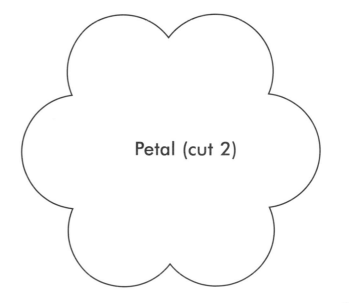

Petal (cut 2)

Stripy Stu

(page 42)

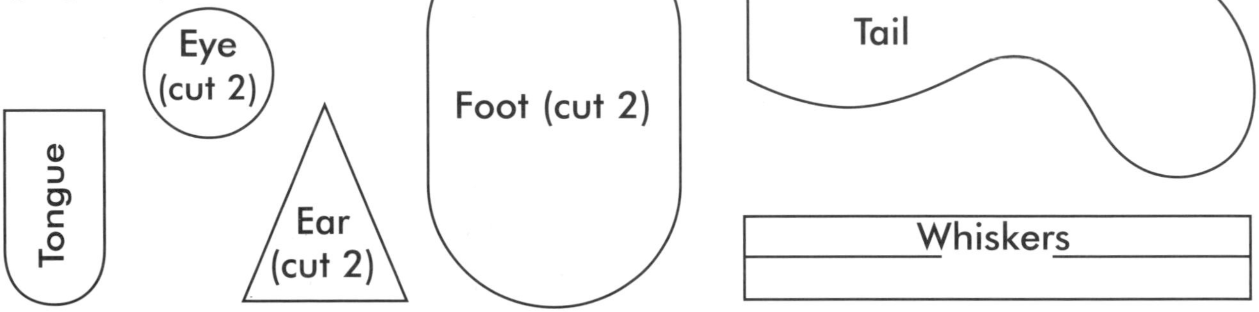

Eye (cut 2)

Tongue

Ear (cut 2)

Foot (cut 2)

Tail

Whiskers

Sweet Mousie

(page 52)

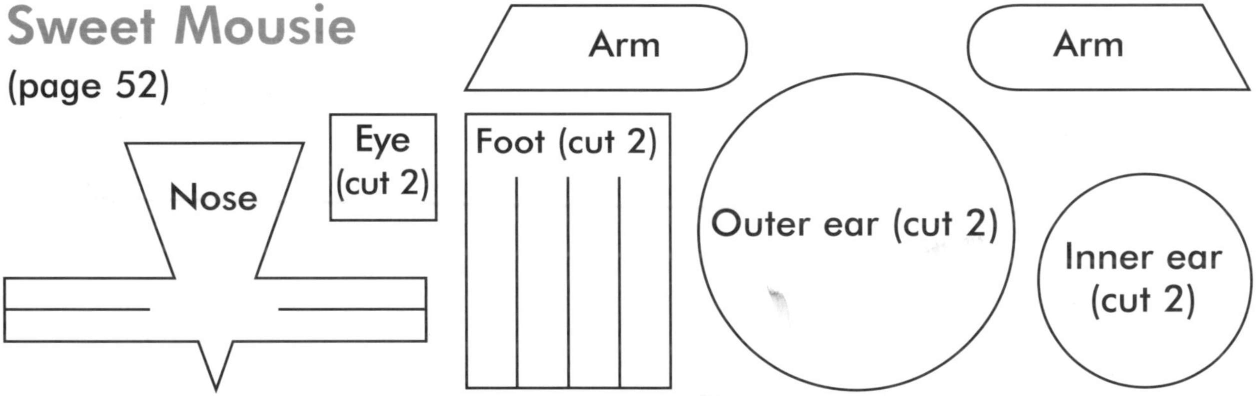

Arm

Arm

Eye (cut 2)

Nose

Foot (cut 2)

Outer ear (cut 2)

Inner ear (cut 2)

All-Together Albert (page 80)

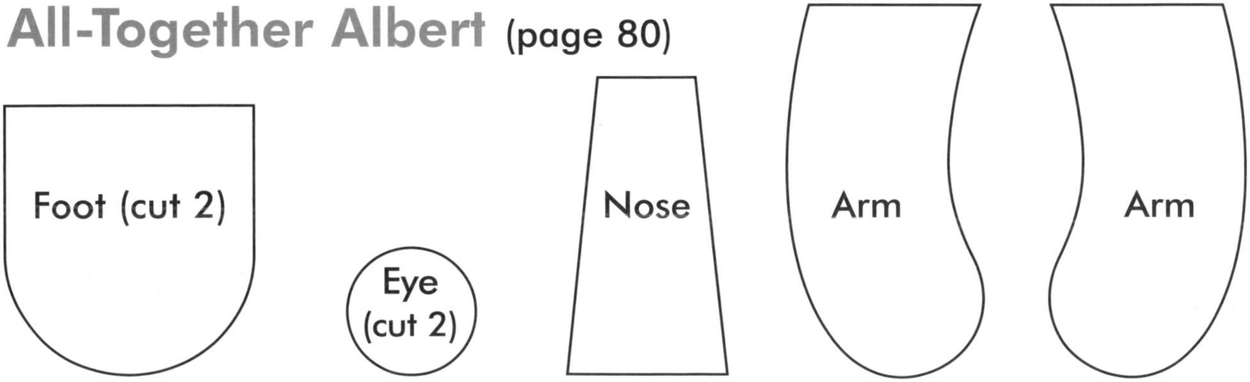

Foot (cut 2)

Eye (cut 2)

Nose

Arm

Arm

YARN INFORMATION

The projects in this book were crocheted in a double-knitting yarn with a 4mm crochet hook. A Patons or Rowan double-knitting yarn in wool or cotton is ideal, but any other yarn that offers the same knitting tension (22 stitches and 30 rows to 10cm measured over stocking stitch using 4mm knitting needles) can be used instead.

For stockists of Patons yarns, contact:
Coats Crafts UK
Lingfield Point
McMullen Road
Darlington
Co. Durham DL1 1YJ
Tel: 01325 394 394
www.coatscrafts.co.uk

For stockists of Rowan yarns, contact:
Rowan Yarns
Green Lane Mill
Holmfirth
West Yorkshire HD9 2DX
Tel: 01484 681 881
www.knitrowan.com

INDEX